Col

By United Library

https://campsite.bio/unitedlibrary

Table of Contents

Disclaimer

This biography book is a work of nonfiction based on the public life of a famous person. The author has used publicly available information to create this work. While the author has thoroughly researched the subject and attempted to depict it accurately, it is not meant to be an exhaustive study of the subject. The views expressed in this book are those of the author alone and do not necessarily reflect those of any organization associated with the subject. This book should not be taken as an endorsement, legal advice, or any other form of professional advice. This book was written for entertainment purposes only.

Introduction

Coldplay invites readers into the captivating world of one of the most successful and influential bands of the 21st century. From their humble beginnings as university friends to their meteoric rise to global stardom, this comprehensive biography explores the fascinating journey of Coldplay.

Formed in London in 1997, Coldplay comprises Chris Martin, Jonny Buckland, Guy Berryman, Will Champion, and creative director Phil Harvey. The book delves into their early days, when they played under various names, including Big Fat Noises and Starfish. It traces their musical evolution, from independently releasing their debut extended play "Safety" in 1998 to signing with Parlophone in 1999.

The band's breakthrough came with their debut album, "Parachutes" (2000), featuring the iconic single "Yellow." The book takes readers through the creation of subsequent albums like "A Rush of Blood to the Head" (2002) and "X&Y" (2005), which solidified their status as major players in the music industry. Coldplay's sound continued to evolve, and their fourth album, "Viva la Vida or Death and All His Friends" (2008), showcased their musical diversity and earned critical acclaim.

"Music of the Spheres" (2021), the band's most recent studio album, marked another chapter in their musical journey, incorporating a fusion of styles ranging from electronica to classical. The book explores the thematic depth of each album, shedding light on the band's creative process and their ability to captivate listeners with their euphoric and immersive live performances.

This book also delves into the band's extraordinary achievements, including 100 million album sales worldwide, record-breaking tours, numerous Brit Award nominations and wins, and their groundbreaking impact on the alternative music scene. The book highlights Coldplay's ability to transcend genres, incorporating elements of pop, rock, R&B, and progressive sounds into their music.

With meticulous research and insightful analysis, this biography provides an intimate look into the personal and professional lives of the band members. It celebrates their artistry, explores their influences, and delves into the stories behind their most beloved songs. "Coldplay: A Musical Odyssey" is an essential read for fans and music enthusiasts alike, offering a comprehensive portrait of a band that has left an indelible mark on the music landscape, inspiring generations with their soulful melodies and thought-provoking lyrics.

Coldplay

Coldplay is a British band formed in London in 1996. It is composed of 5 members: Chris Martin (lead vocalist and pianist), Jonny Buckland (guitarist), Guy Berryman (bassist), Will Champion (drummer and backing vocalist) and Phil Harvey (creative director). They met at University College London and began playing music together from 1997 to 1998, initially calling themselves Big Fat Noises and then Starfish.

After independently releasing an EP, *Safety* (1998), Coldplay signed with Parlophone in 1999. The band's debut album, *Parachutes* (2000), included their hit single "Yellow" and received a Brit Award for British Album of the Year, a Grammy Award for Best Alternative Music Album and a Mercury Prize nomination. Their second album, *A Rush of Blood to the Head* (2002), won the same accolades and included the singles "The Scientist" and "Clocks," and the latter won a Grammy Award for Record of the Year. Notable for a troubled production, the band's third album, *X&Y* (2005), was the best-selling album of the year worldwide, an achievement repeated by its successor, *Viva la Vida or Death and All His Friends* (2008), which saw them explore new musical styles. territory after the completion of what was considered a trilogy. It received a Grammy Award for Best Rock Album and their first nomination for Album of the Year, while the title track became the first single by a British group to reach number one in both the UK and the US in the 21st century.

Since then, Coldplay further diversified their sound with subsequent releases *Mylo Xyloto* (2011), *Ghost Stories* (2014), *A Head Full of Dreams* (2015), *Everyday Life* (2019) and *Music of the Spheres* (2021). Each album featured a unique track and added new musical styles to the band's original repertoire, including electronica, *ambient*, pop, R&B, *funk*, classical, *jazz* fusion and progressive *rock.* They are also known for their "euphoric" live performances, which *NME* said is when the band "comes alive and makes the most sense." To celebrate their 20th anniversary in 2018, a career-spanning documentary directed by Mat Whitecross, featuring never-before-seen behind-the-scenes footage, was released in select theaters.

With 100 million albums sold worldwide, Coldplay is the most successful band of the 21st century and one of the best-selling musical acts of all time. According to Fuse, they are also the sixth most awarded band in history. Other notable achievements include the sixth highest-grossing tour of all time, three of the top 50 best-selling albums in the UK, the most number one albums in the country without ever losing the top spot, the most nominations and wins for a band in Brit Awards history and becoming the first British group to debut at number one on the *Billboard* Hot 100. Coldplay is also considered one of the most influential bands of the 21st century, and Forbes describes them as the standard. for today's alternative scene. The Rock and Roll Hall of Fame included *A Rush of Blood to the Head* in their "200 Ultimate Albums" list and the single "Yellow" is part of their "Songs That Shaped Rock and Roll" showcase for being one of the most successful and important recordings in the industry. Despite their popularity and impact, Coldplay have earned a reputation for being polarizing musical icons.

History

1996-1999: training and early years

Chris Martin and Jonny Buckland met during their orientation week at University College London in September 1996. The pair began writing their first songs together in late 1996 and practiced every night. Guy Berryman was the third member to join the band in the following months and they recorded several demos without a drummer, calling themselves Starfish in November.In 1997, Will Champion completed the formation of Starfish. He explained that Martin, Buckland and Berryman had come to his house because a roommate had a drum kit and was a good drummer, but hadn't shown up, "so I said I'd give it a try."

Champion scheduled the band's first live performance just a few days after joining the band. The band was then called Starfish. In 1998 it was decided to change the name to Coldplay, and under that name the band released *Safety*, an independent extended play financed by Martin's lifelong friend Phil Harvey. Of the 500 copies printed, 150 went to the open market. Harvey sold the first one to his roommate for £3 and the rest were given away to record labels.

When Martin complained about the "almost vicious control" that one of the Camden promoters had over the band, Harvey suggested that the group should book their own gig at Dingwalls, where they managed to sell 50 copies of *Safety*. From this point onwards it is believed that Harvey began to act as Coldplay's manager and then abandoned his degree in Classical Studies at Trinity College, Oxford to work. More gigs were scheduled during the summer, including two with Keane. Once, Martin invited Tim Rice-Oxley to be Coldplay's keyboard player, but "when we discussed it again a couple of weeks later, he said the rest of the band wasn't interested in bringing in a member."In September 1998, they were part of the In the City showcase in Manchester and were discovered by A&R talent scout Debs Wild. *Safety was* followed by a cassette mauqeta with "Ode to Deodorant" and "Brothers & Sisters".

Wild informed Caroline Elleray of BMG Publishing and music lawyer Gavin Maude about the band. The former spoke to Dan Keeling at Parlophone but he had already passed them up. Meanwhile, the latter spoke to Simon Williams of Fierce Panda Records, who in turn told BBC Radio's Steve Lamacq. On January 3, 1999, Coldplay became the first unsigned act to invite to Lamacq's evening session.A month later, they did a brief deal with Fierce Panda and re-recorded "Brothers & Sisters. "Six other labels offered a contract as the band's popularity grew, but they wanted Parlophone, prompting Elleray to contact Keeling once again.He changed his mind and the deal was signed in Trafalgar Square in April 1999, the same month "Brothers & Sisters" was released as a single.The next few days were spent studying for final exams at UCL.

On June 27, 1999, Coldplay made their first appearance at the Glastonbury Festival in the New Bands Tent. They later recorded *The Blue Room*, which had 5 000 copies printed and sold to the public. Their sessions were originally intended for *Parachutes* (2000), but ended up becoming tumultuous, as Martin and Champion had heated arguments over the latter's drumming skills: "Three days later, the rest of us were miserable, [...] we asked him to come back. They made me drink a lot of vodka and cranberry juice as a reminder of how unpleasant I was proving to be to work with." After resolving their differences, the band began to work as a democracy, established a new set of rules and declared that anyone using hard drugs would be expelled from the group immediately, a decision inspired by R.E.M. and U2 rules.

2000-2001: *Parachutes*

The band first planned to record their debut album, *Parachutes*, within two weeks. However, due to touring and other live performances, recording took place between September 1999 and April-May 2000. The album was recorded at Rockfield Studios, Matrix Studios and Wessex Sound Studios with producer Ken Nelson, although most of the tracks on *Parachutes* were recorded at Parr Street Studios, Liverpool - where they used three studio rooms - and American engineer Michael Brauer in New York mixed all the songs on the album. American engineer Michael Brauer in New York mixed all the songs on the album, during which time they played on the Carling Tour, which showcased promising acts.

After releasing two EPs without a hit song, Coldplay had their first Top 40 hit with *Parachutes*' lead single, "Shiver", released in March 2000, the same week Coldplay played at The Forum in Tunbridge Wells supporting the band Terris as part of the *NME* Premier Tour."Shiver" peaked at number 35 on the UK Singles Chart. June 2000 was a pivotal moment in Coldplay's history: the band embarked on their first headline tour, including a performance at Glastonbury Festival. The band also released the single "Yellow"; it was Coldplay's first release to reach the top five and climbed to number four on the UK Singles Chart.The minimalist music video for "Yellow" was filmed in Studland Bay, Dorset and featured Martin singing the song in one continuous take while walking along the beach. "Yellow" and "Shiver" were initially released as an EP in the spring of 2000.The former was later released as a single in the UK on June 26, 2000. In the United States, the song released, as the lead single from the debut album, was untitled. In October 2000, the track was sent to U.S. colleges and alternative radio stations.

Coldplay released *Parachutes* on July 10, 2000 in the United Kingdom through their record label, Parlophone. The album debuted at number one on the UK album chart. It was released on November 7, 2000 by the Nettwerk record label in North America. The album has been available in various formats since its initial release; both Parlophone and Nettwerk released it as a CD in 2000, and it was also released as a cassette by the U.S. label Capitol in 2001. The following year, Parlophone released the album as an LP. Four *Parachutes* singles were released, including "Shiver" and "Yellow", and enjoyed popularity in the U.K. and U.S. The third single was "Trouble", which reached number 10 in the U.K. charts.It was released over a year later in the U.S. and reached #28 on the Alternative Songs chart. In December 2001, the band released a limited edition CD, *Mince Spies*, with a *remix* of "Yellow" and the Christmas song "Have Yourself a Merry Little Christmas". 1,000 copies were printed and issued to fans and journalists only.

Parachutes was nominated for the Mercury Music Prize in September 2000. Having found success in Europe, the band set its sights on North America, releasing the album there in November 2000, and began the US Club Tour in

February 2001. At the 2001 Brit Awards in February, Coldplay won awards for Best British Group and Best British Album. Although *Parachutes* was a slow success in the United States, it eventually achieved double platinum status.The album was well received by critics and won Best Alternative Music Album at the 2002 Grammy Awards. Chris Martin said after the release of *Parachutes* that the album's success was destined to elevate the band's status to "the biggest and best band in the world." After managing the band by himself until early 2001, Harvey resigned due to the stress of having to perform tasks that normally require a team of people. He became the band's creative director and is often referred to as its fifth member; Dave Holmes replaced him as manager.

2002-2004: *A Rush of Blood to the Head*

After the success of *Parachutes*, Coldplay returned to the studio in September 2001 to begin work on their second album, *A Rush of Blood to the Head*, once again with Ken Nelson producing. They had trouble concentrating in London and decided to move to Liverpool, where they recorded some of the songs at *Parachutes*. Once there, vocalist Chris Martin said they became obsessed with recording. "In My Place" was the first song recorded for the album. The band released it as the lead single from the album because it was the track that made them want to record a second album, after a "weird period of not really knowing what we were doing" three months after the success of *Parachutes*. According to Martin, "one thing kept us going: recording "In My Place." Then other songs started coming in."

The band wrote more than twenty songs for the album. Some of their new material, including "In My Place" and "Animals", was played live while the band was still touring with *Parachutes*. The album title was revealed through a posting on the band's official website. The album was released in August 2002 and spawned several popular singles, including "In My Place", "Clocks" and the ballad "The Scientist". The latter was inspired by George Harrison's "All Things Must Pass," which was released in 1970.

Coldplay toured from June 19, 2002 to September 8, 2003 for the A Rush of Blood to the Head Tour. They visited five continents, including co-headlining festival dates at Glastonbury Festival, V2003 and Rock Werchter. Many concerts featured elaborate lighting and individualized screens reminiscent of U2's Elevation Tour and Nine Inch Nails' Fragility Tour. During the extended tour, Coldplay recorded a live DVD and CD, *Live 2003*, at Sydney's Hordern Pavilion.At the 2003 Brit Awards held at Earls Court, London, Coldplay received awards for Best British Group and Best British Album. On August 28, 2003, Coldplay performed "The Scientist" at the 2003 MTV

Video Music Awards at Radio City Music Hall in New York City and won three awards.

In December 2003, readers of *Rolling Stone* magazine chose Coldplay as the best artist and best band of the year. At the time, the band performed a cover of the Pretenders' 1983 song "2000 Miles" - which was available for download on their official website. "2000 Miles" was the best-selling download in the U.K. that year, and proceeds from sales were donated to the Future Forests and Stop Handgun Violence campaigns. *A Rush of Blood to the Head* won the Grammy Award for Best Alternative Music Album at the 2003 Grammy Awards. At the 2004 Grammy Awards, Coldplay won Record of the Year for "Clocks."

2005-2007: *X&Y*

Coldplay spent most of 2004 out of the spotlight, taking a break from touring and releasing a satirical music video for a song by a fictional band titled The Nappies while recording their third album, *X&Y*, released in June 2005 in the U.K. and Europe. This new delayed release date had put the album back into the next fiscal year, and the late release was blamed for a drop in EMI's stock.It became the best-selling album of 2005 with worldwide sales of 8.3 million. The lead single, "Speed of Sound", made its radio and online music store debut on April 18 and was released as a CD on May 23, 2005. *X&Y* entered the album charts in 20 countries at number one and was the third best-selling album in UK chart history.

Two more singles were released that year: "Fix You" in September and "Talk" in December. Critical reaction to *X&Y* was mostly positive, if slightly less enthusiastic than that of its predecessor. *New York Times* critic Jon Pareles infamously described Coldplay as "the most insufferable band of the decade," while *NME* awarded the album 9/10 calling it "Confident, bold, ambitious, full of singles and impossible to contain, *X&Y* doesn't reinvent the wheel but it does reinforce Coldplay as the band of their time."Comparisons between Coldplay and U2 became commonplace. Martin said the *New York Times*' critical review of the album made him feel liberated as he "agreed with many of the points," adding that "in a way, it was liberating to see that someone else realized that too."

From June 2005 to March 2007, Coldplay performed their Twisted Logic Tour, which included festivals such as Coachella, Isle of Wight Festival, Glastonbury and Austin City Limits Music Festival. In July 2005, the band appeared at Hyde Park's Live 8, where they played a cover of The Verve's "Bitter Sweet Symphony" with Richard Ashcroft on vocals.On August 28, Coldplay performed "Speed of Sound" at the 2005 MTV Video Music Awards in Miami. In September, Coldplay recorded a new version of "How You

See the World" with reworked lyrics for the charity album *War Child's Help!: A Day in the Life*. In February 2006, Coldplay won Best Album and Best Single honors at the Brit Awards. Three more singles were released during 2006 and 2007, "The Hardest Part", "What If" and "White Shadows".

2008-2010: *Viva la Vida or Death and All His Friends*

In October 2006, Coldplay began work on their fourth studio album, *Viva la Vida or Death and All His Friends*, with producer Brian Eno. While taking a break from recording, the band toured Latin America in early 2007, where they completed the Twisted Logic Tour while performing in Chile, Argentina, Brazil and Mexico. After recording in churches and other venues in Latin America and Spain during their tour, the band said the album would likely reflect the Hispanic influence. The group spent the rest of the year recording most of the album with Eno.

Martin described *Viva la Vida as* a new direction for Coldplay; a departure from their last three albums, which the band felt was a "trilogy" they had completed. He said the album featured less falsetto, as he allowed the lower register of his voice to take precedence. Some songs, such as "Violet Hill," contain distorted guitar *riffs* and *blues* overtones.

"Violet Hill" was confirmed as the first single, with a radio release date of April 29, 2008. After the first play, it was available for free on Coldplay's website from 12:15 p.m. (GMT +0) for a week until it became commercially available on May 6. "Violet Hill" entered the UK *top* 10, the U.S. *top* 40 and placed well in the rest of the world, The title track, "Viva la Vida," also released exclusively on iTunes, became the band's first number one on both the U.S. *Billboard* Hot 100 and the official U.K. charts. Coldplay performed the song live for the first time at the 2008 MTV Movie Awards on June 1. "Viva la Vida" became the best-selling song on iTunes in 2008.

Upon its release, *Viva la Vida or Death and All His Friends* topped the album charts worldwide and became the world's best-selling album in 2008, reaching number one on the UK Singles Chart despite having been released only three days earlier, selling 302,000 copies in that time, making it "one of the best-selling albums in the country's history. In that time it sold 302,000 copies, making it "one of the best-selling albums in the country's history". By the end of June, it had set a new record for the most downloaded album in history. In October 2008, Coldplay won two Q Awards for Best Album for *Viva la Vida or Death and All His Friends* and Best Performance in Today's World.On November 9, Coldplay was named the World's Best Selling Act of 2008 at the World Music Awards in Monte Carlo. They also picked up two other awards:

World's Best Selling Rock Act and Britain's Best Selling Act. The band followed *Viva la Vida or Death and All His Friends* with the EP *Prospekt's March*, released on November 21, 2008. The extended playback features songs from the album sessions and was originally available on its own, while the album was reissued with all the tracks from the EP included on a bonus disc. "Life in Technicolor II" was the only single released.

Coldplay kicked off their Viva la Vida Tour in June with a free concert at London's Brixton Academy. This was followed two days later by a 45-minute performance that was broadcast live from outside the BBC Television Centre. Released in late 2008, "Lost!" became the third single from the album, with a new version featuring Jay-Z called "Lost+". After performing the opening set on March 14, 2009 for Sound Relief at the Sydney Cricket Ground, Coldplay headlined a sold-out concert later that night. Sound Relief is a benefit concert for victims of the Victorian bushfire crisis and the Queensland floods. On December 4, 2008, Joe Satriani filed a copyright infringement lawsuit against Coldplay in the United States District Court for the Central District of California. Satriani's lawsuit claimed that Coldplay's song "Viva La Vida" includes "substantial original portions" of Satriani's song "If I Could Fly" from his 2004 album, *Is There Love in Space?* The Coldplay song in question received two Grammy Awards for "Song of the Year." The band denied the allegation. Eventually, an unspecified settlement was reached between the parties.

Coldplay was nominated for four awards at the 2009 Brit Awards: British Group, British Live Act, British Single - "Viva la Vida"- and British Album -Viva *la Vida or Death and All His Friends*-.At the 51st Grammy Awards that same year, Coldplay won three Grammy Awards in the categories Song of the Year for "Viva la Vida", Best Rock Album for *Viva la Vida or Death and All His Friends* and Best Pop Vocal Performance by a Duo or Group for "Viva la Vida". A live album entitled *LeftRightLeftRightLeft* was recorded at various shows during the tour. *LeftRightLeftLeftRightLeft*, released on May 15, 2009, would be given away at the remaining concerts of their Viva la Vida Tour. It was released as a free download from their website. Following the Viva La Vida Tour, Coldplay announced another "Latin American tour" to take place in February and March 2010, visiting Mexico, Argentina, Brazil and Colombia. In October 2009, Coldplay won Song of the Year for "Viva La Vida" at the American Society of Composers, Authors and Publishers (ASCAP) awards in London.In December 2009, *Rolling Stone* readers voted the group as the fourth best artist of the 2000s, and they were also included in *Q*'s Artist of the Century List. *In* December 2010, the band released "Christmas Lights". The song received rave reviews and the music video features a cameo by actor Simon Pegg, a close friend of

Chris Martin, who plays an Elvis impersonator fiddling in the background.

2011-2012: *Mylo Xyloto*

The band finished recording the new album in mid-2011. When Martin and Champion were interviewed by BBC Radio and asked about the album's lyrical themes, Martin replied, "It's about love, addiction, OCD, escape and working for someone you don't like." When asked whether or not their fifth album would be out by the summer, Martin and Champion said there was a lot of work to be done before releasing it. They confirmed several festival appearances ahead of its release date, including a headlining spot at 2011's Glastonbury Festival, T in the Park, Austin City Limits Music Festival, Rock in Rio, and the Lollapalooza festival.

In an interview on January 13, 2011, Coldplay mentioned that two new songs would be included on their upcoming fifth album, "Princess of China" and "Every Teardrop Is a Waterfall". In an interview in February, Parlophone president Miles Leonard told HitQuarters that the band was still in the studio working on the album and that he expected the final version to appear "around autumn this year". On May 31, 2011, Coldplay announced that "Every Teardrop Is a Waterfall" was the first single from the fifth album. It was released on June 3, 2011. The band performed five new songs at festivals during the summer of 2011, "Charlie Brown", "Hurts Like Heaven", "Us Against the World", "Princess of China" and "Major Minus".

On August 12, 2011, Coldplay announced through its official website that *Mylo Xyloto* was the title of the new album and would be released on October 24, 2011. On September 12, 2011, the band released "Paradise", the second single from their upcoming album *Mylo Xyloto*. On September 23, 2011, tickets for Coldplay's European tour officially went on sale. Demand proved to be very high and most venues sold out within seconds. *Mylo Xyloto* was released on October 24, 2011, received positive reviews and topped the charts in over 34 countries.

On October 19, 2011, Coldplay performed songs at Apple Inc.'s private memorial for Steve Jobs, including "Viva la Vida", "Fix You", "Yellow" and "Every Teardrop Is a Waterfall". On October 26, their "Amex Unstaged" concert at the Plaza de Toros de Las Ventas in Madrid, Spain, was broadcast on YouTube as a live *webcast* directed by Anton Corbijn.On November 30, 2011, Coldplay received three Grammy nominations for the 54th Annual Grammy Awards, which took place on February 12, 2012 in Los Angeles, and the band performed with Rihanna at the ceremony.On January 12, 2012, Coldplay was nominated for two Brit Awards. On February 21, 2012, they received the Brit Award for Best

British Group for the third time. *Mylo Xyloto became the* best-selling *rock* album in the UK, selling 908,000 copies.The album's second single, "Paradise", was also the best-selling *rock* single in the UK, selling 410,000 copies. At the 2012 MTV Video Music Awards, "Paradise" won the award for Best Rock Video. *Mylo Xyloto* has sold more than 8 million copies worldwide.

Coldplay headlined the closing ceremony of the London 2012 Paralympic Games on September 9, 2012, where they performed alongside other artists such as Rihanna and Jay-Z. To coincide with their performance at the closing ceremony, the group gave permission for bands participating in the Bandstand Marathon to perform their 2008 single "Viva la Vida" to celebrate the end of the games.

In October 2012, the music video for Coldplay's song "Hurts Like Heaven" was released. The video was based on the story of Mylo Xyloto, a boy growing up in the tyranny led by Major Minus. Fictional comics titled *Mylo Xyloto* continued the story portrayed in the music video when the series was released in early 2013. A concert documentary film and live album *Coldplay Live 2012* chronicles their tour in support of the *Mylo Xyloto* album. The film was released in theaters one night only on November 13, 2012, and was released on CD and home video on November 19, 2012.

On November 21, following a concert in Brisbane, Australia, as part of the group's Mylo Xyloto Tour, Coldplay hinted that they would be taking a three-year break from touring. Coldplay performed two shows with Jay-Z at the Barclays Center, Brooklyn, New York, on December 30 and New Year's Eve, which ended the Mylo Xyloto tour. The Mylo Xyloto tour was named the fourth highest grossing tour worldwide in 2012 with more than $171.3 million earned in ticket sales.

2013-2014: *Ghost Stories*

In an interview with Australian radio station 2Day FM, Chris Martin revealed that the title of the band's next album would be "a lot easier to pronounce." Martin debunked speculation that they were taking a break from touring by saying, "This idea of a three-year break only came about because I said at a gig in Australia that we might not be back there for three years. That's probably true, but that's just how a world tour works. There's no chance we're going to take a three-year break."

On August 9, 2013, Coldplay announced the release of their song "Atlas", which appeared on the soundtrack of the film *The Hunger Games: Catching Fire*. Its release was delayed until September 6, 2013 -everywhere but the UK- and September 8 -UK-. In December 2013, it was announced that future Coldplay releases would be distributed by Atlantic Records in the U.S. due to restructuring within Warner Music Group following the purchase of Parlophone Records from EMI.

On February 25, 2014, the band unveiled "Midnight," a track from their yet-to-be-released album. In early March 2014, it was announced that the band's sixth album, *Ghost Stories*, would be released on May 19, 2014. *Ghost Stories* is a spiritually driven album that revolves around two main themes mentioned by Chris Martin. The album explores the idea of past actions and the effects they can have on the future and one's capacity for unconditional love. The band took a different approach for their sixth studio album in contrast to their previous studio albums, with Martin inviting the band to contribute original songwriting material for the album, rather than building songs from their ideas as they had done during previous recording sessions.

From April through July, Coldplay embarked on a six-date Ghost Stories Tour in support of the album, playing "intimate" shows in six cities: the Beacon Theatre in New York City on May 5, Royce Hall in Los Angeles on May 19, Casino de Paris in Paris on May 28, Tokyo Dome City Hall in Tokyo on June 12, Enmore Theatre in Sydney on June 19 and closed the tour at London's Royal Albert Hall on July 2, 2014.The album was available for pre-order on iTunes, along with the new single "Magic." Since then, two more singles from the album, "A Sky Full of Stars" and

"True Love," have been released. *Ghost Stories* received mixed to positive reviews. The album topped the charts in the U.K., U.S. and most major markets. It received a Grammy Award nomination for Best Pop Vocal Album, and "A Sky Full of Stars" was nominated for Best Pop Duo/Group Performance. In December 2014, Spotify named Coldplay the most played band in the world in 2014 and the third most played artist behind Ed Sheeran and Eminem.

2015-2018: *A Head Full of Dreams*

On December 4, 2014, Chris Martin announced in an interview with Zane Lowe on BBC Radio 1 that Coldplay was working on their seventh studio album, *A Head Full of Dreams*. Martin commented that it could be the band's final album and compared it to *Harry Potter*: "It's our seventh thing, and the way we look at it, it's like the last *Harry Potter* book or something."He added that unlike their promotional efforts for *Ghost Stories*, the band will tour the seventh album. In an interview with Jo Whiley on BBC Radio 2, Martin hinted at the style of the album by saying that the band was trying to do something colorful and uplifting, but not grandiloquent. He also stated that it will be something to "move the feet".

On December 11, 2014, the band unveiled a new song, "Miracles," which was written and recorded for the World War II drama film *Unbroken* directed by Angelina Jolie. At the 2015 Billboard Music Awards on May 17, *Ghost Stories* was named Best Rock Album.On September 26, Coldplay performed at the 2015 Global Citizen Festival at the Great Lawn in Central Park in New York, an event organized by Chris Martin that advocates for an end to extreme poverty in the world. Coldplay, along with Beyoncé, Ed Sheeran and Pearl Jam, headlined the festival which aired on NBC in the U.S. on September 27 and on BBC in the U.K. on September 28.

Speaking on Nick Grimshaw's *Radio 1 Breakfast Show* on the BBC on November 6, Coldplay confirmed December 4 as the release date for *A Head Full of Dreams*, and a new song from the album, "Adventure of a Lifetime" premiered on the show. The album features special appearances from Beyoncé, Gwyneth Paltrow, Noel Gallagher, Tove Lo and Barack Obama. The album reached number one in the UK and number two in the U.S., Australia and Canada, among others, where Adele's 25 held number two, Australia and Canada, among others, where Adele's *25* kept it in second place. The music video for "Adventure of a Lifetime" featured the band performing as chimpanzees. They were provided consultation with renowned motion capture actor Andy Serkis.

On November 27, 2015, the first dates for his 2016 A Head Full of Dreams Tour were announced. Latin

American and European stops were listed, which included three dates at Wembley Stadium, London, in June. The North American tour, an additional Wembley concert and an Oceania tour were later added. On December 5, the band headlined the opening day of the 2015 Jingle Bell Ball at London's O2 Arena. On February 7, 2016, they headlined the Super Bowl 50 halftime show, and were joined by Beyoncé and Bruno Mars. In April 2016, the band was named the sixth best-selling artist worldwide in 2015.

On June 26, 2016, Coldplay closed out the final day of the Glastonbury Festival in England. Their performance included a duet with Barry Gibb, the last surviving member of the Bee Gees. During the band's second night at MetLife Stadium in New Jersey on July 18, Michael J. Fox joined Coldplay on stage to recreate a scene from *Back to the Future*. Martin sang "Earth Angel" before introducing Fox on stage to join the band for a rendition of the Chuck Berry classic "Johnny B. Goode."

The band performed a full set in India for the first time as part of the Global Citizen Festival in Mumbai on November 19, 2016. This performance was attended by 80 000 people and also featured many Bollywood stars during the concert. The same month, Coldplay announced in interviews with Absolute Radio and Magic Radio in London that they would be releasing new songs on a new

EP called *Kaleidoscope EP*. Described as being made from a "bag of ideas" left over from the recording of *A Head Full of Dreams*, Martin stated that it would be released in "a couple of months." The band officially announced that the EP was released on July 14, 2017.

On February 22, 2017, the band released a long-awaited collaborative track with EDM duo The Chainsmokers called "Something Just Like This." Reaching No. 2 on the UK Singles Chart and No. 3 on the U.S. *Billboard* Hot 100, it was the lead single from Coldplay's thirteenth extended play, *Kaleidoscope*, released on July 14, 2017. Together, they debuted the song live at the 2017 Brit Awards with Chris. Martin also performed a tribute song to the late George Michael. On March 2, Martin's birthday, the band released a song from the EP, "Hypnotised." Two more releases from the EP, "All I Can Think About Is You" and "Aliens," came out on June 15 and July 6, 2017 respectively. On August 15, 2017, Coldplay announced that a live album covering the A Head Full of Dreams Tour would be released.

On October 8, 2017, Coldplay debuted their new song called "Life Is Beautiful" live at SDCCU Stadium in San Diego, California. It was written in support after the earthquake that hit Mexico on September 19. Part of the band's show aired at the end of Estamos Unidos Mexicanos, a benefit concert held in Mexico City's Zocalo, which included "Fix You," "Viva la Vida," "Adventure of a Lifetime" and their new song. Martin stated that proceeds from the song and concert would be donated to relief efforts for Mexico and other countries.

The A Head Full of Dreams Tour came to an end in November 2017. Grossing over $523 million, in 2017 it was ranked as the third highest grossing concert tour of all time. The promised live album, which is titled *Live in Buenos Aires*, was released on December 7, 2018. Its footage covers the final concert of the tour in La Plata and a second release called *Love in Tokyo* was available at the same time exclusively for the Japanese market. On November 30, 2018, Coldplay released *Global Citizen - EP 1* under the name Los Unidades. It includes "E-Lo", a song with Pharrell Williams and Jozzy. Proceeds from the EP were donated to efforts to end global poverty.

2019-2020: *Everyday Life*

On September 26, 2019, Global Citizen announced that Coldplay would perform at Global Goal Live: The Possible Dream on September 26, 2020. On October 18, 2019, mysterious black and white posters began appearing in various countries around the world, featuring the band in *vintage-style* clothing and a date showing November 22, 1919. The band also changed their profile pictures on social media to a sun and a moon, causing fans to speculate about an imminent release of new material. On

October 19, 2019, a cryptic 5-second *teaser* was posted on social media with orchestral music in the background. On October 21, 2019, in a letter sent to fans, the band announced that their eighth studio album would be titled *Everyday Life* and that it would be a double album, with the first half titled *Sunrise* and the second half titled *Sunset.*

On October 23, 2019, tracks from the album were revealed in advertisements in the band members' local UK newspapers, including the Daily Post in North Wales - with whom Jonny Buckland once had a vacation job - and Exeter's Express & Echo - Chris Martin's hometown newspaper."Orphans" and "Arabesque" were released as the album's lead singles on October 24, 2019 on Annie Mac's BBC Radio 1 show, with the latter song being the first Coldplay song to feature profanity. The album was released on November 22, 2019 and was marked by a double concert in Amman, Jordan. The concert, which was streamed live to YouTube, took place at sunrise and sunset, corresponding with the subtitles of the album's two halves.

Martin had previously said that the band would not tour to promote the album until they could work out "how our tour can not only be sustainable - but - how it can be actively beneficial," and he hopes it will be completely carbon neutral. However, Coldplay did perform a one-off show on November 25, 2019 for the charity ClientEarth at London's Natural History Museum. The band played under Hope, a giant skeleton of a 128-year-old blue whale in the museum's great hall. The album debuted at number one on the UK Albums Chart with 81 000 copies sold, making it the band's eighth consecutive number one album in the UK. It was also the third fastest-selling album of 2019, behind *No. 6 Collaborations Project* and *Divinely Uninspired to a Hellish Extent*. On November 24, 2020, Coldplay received two nominations for the 63rd annual Grammy Awards, one of them being Album of the Year, their first nomination in the category since *Viva la Vida*. On December 21, 2020, "Flags" was released internationally, the song was originally included as a Japanese bonus track on *Everyday Life*.

2021-present: *Music of the Spheres*

On April 29, 2021, Coldplay announced a new single called "Higher Power" to be released on May 7, 2021 with a live video stream that coincided with the release of the single being broadcast from the International Space Station. Chris Martin stated in an interview with Zane Lowe that the band would be working with Max Martin and his team on both the song and the new album. He said, "Max is our producer at the moment for everything we do." On May 4, 2021, Coldplay was announced as the opening act for the 2021 Brit Awards, where they would perform "Higher Power."

On May 22, 2021, their pre-recorded performance at the Glastonbury Festival was streamed online. The band also unveiled a new song called "Human Heart", featuring R&B duo We Are King. On June 8, 2021, the "official" music video for "Higher Power", directed by Dave Meyers, was released on YouTube, following a simpler music video in which the band performs the song while dancing with CGI alien holograms that was released on May 7, 2021.On July 20, 2021, Coldplay announced that its new album *Music of the Spheres* would be released on October 15, 2021 and also announced a song titled "Coloratura," released on July 23, 2021.

On September 13, 2021, they announced with South Korean *K-pop* group BTS the second single, "My Universe", released on September 24, 2021. The song debuted at number 3 on the UK Singles Chart, being their highest peaking single since "Something Just Like This" and then debuted at number one on the *Billboard* Hot 100 in the U.S. Subsequently, on September 26, 2021, a short documentary about the collaboration with BTS was released on the said band's official YouTube channel.

Music of the Spheres debuted at number one on the UK Albums Chart, becoming the best-selling album in the country since Ed Sheeran's *No. 6 Collaborations Project* in

2019. The album debuted at number four on the U.S. *Billboard* 200 chart and reached number one on the Top Alternative Albums and Top Rock Albums charts. On October 14, 2021, Coldplay announced its eighth concert tour, the *Music of the Spheres* world tour, which will kick off in San Jose, Costa Rica in March 2022 and visit three continents, with more dates to be announced in the future.The tour is part of an ongoing effort to reduce the band's carbon footprint; Chris Martin explained in an interview with the BBC that the tour would feature "kinetic floors" that power concerts through the movement of attendees, as well as bicycles that do the same, meaning "the whole show runs on renewable energy." Martin said the band's goal is that they will have "slightly changed the status quo of how a tour works." On Nov. 23, 2021, "Higher Power" was nominated for Best Pop Duo/Group Performance at the 64th Annual Grammy Awards. In December 2021, Martin said Coldplay would release three more albums through 2025 during an interview for the BBC, with one of them being "a kind of musical," while the last will be a "back-to-basics" eponymous album.He added, however, that the band will remain active with smaller releases and world tours after 2025. On February 23, 2022, the band released a new, simplified version of "Let Somebody Go" and a cover of Kid Cudi's 2008 single "Day 'n' Nite." Both songs were part of their Spotify Singles release. The album received three nominations at the 65th Annual Grammy Awards announced on November 15, 2022, including Album of the Year and Best Pop Vocal Album, and "My Universe" was nominated for Best Pop Duo/Group Performance.

Creative process

Bassist Guy Berryman once explained that the band often has a title and concept in mind before the music arrives, which serves to provide a "framework that we can work within thematically."During a 2019 YouTube interview, lead vocalist Chris Martin described their songwriting as "a series of doors" where he generally contributes initial ideas to guitarist Jonny Buckland, who either disapproves or gives feedback on them. The same happens from Buckland to Berryman and then to drummer Will Champion, which allows each band member to express themselves artistically. However, it is known that this process is not always linear, given that tracks like "Magic" and "Adventure of a Lifetime" began with Berryman and Buckland's bass and guitar *riffs* respectively. When asked about avoiding the use of explicit language in lyrics, Champion mentioned that "sometimes there are more elegant ways to say something" and "swear words are extremely useful at times," but "if you overuse them, it lessens their impact."

Critics also noted a pattern whereby the band alternated "between overt bids for mainstream success and more artful, conscious prestige pieces." Buckland commented, "Knowing that the big [album] is coming allows us to be much smaller" and "be much more insular about what music we make sense of." They are also known to try different aesthetics for the promotion of each album, with James Hall of *The Telegraph* citing how, over the years, Coldplay's appearance "has morphed from skinny *indie* kids [*Parachutes*] to chorus members of *Les Misérables* [*Viva la Vida or Death and All His Friends*], to a sepia-tinted *jazz* band from 1919 [*Everyday Life*]."After being questioned about the black attire and white shoes worn by the group while promoting *X&Y* (2005), Martin added on the matter saying, "There's a great security in looking at [Buckland] and seeing that he's wearing the same color shoes as me. I guess it's the same reason the military wears uniforms, to make you feel like you're part of a clan. And when we're all dressed that way, I feel like [everything] is right, because I'm part of this team."

Musical and lyrical style

Coldplay has explored many musical styles throughout their career, and their sound is considered alternative *rock*, alternative pop, pop *rock, post-britpop, soft rock,* and pop. After winning a Grammy Award for Best Rock Album in 2009, Martin jokingly said in his acceptance speech that they were "limestone *rock*" as opposed to "*hard rock*". In the late 1990s, the EPs released by the band had *dream* pop characteristics, differentiating them from future releases. Their first studio album, *Parachutes* (2000), was described as "melodic pop" that combined "bits of distorted guitar *riffs* and whistling percussion," while also being "exquisitely dark and artistically abrasive."Berryman called it "a quiet, polite record," and Champion compared the lyrics to Lou Reed's "Perfect Day," saying they are "quite moody" but with "twists that imply optimism," making them ultimately "beautiful and happy" while the music is "very, very sad." He added that it's the "kind of thing where you can create different moods through sound and lyrics."

2002's *A Rush of Blood to the Head,* on the other hand, is full of "plaintive strumming and tired arpeggios," along with a sense of urgency and angst. During an interview, Martin commented that the album's title means "doing something on impulse."Critics described it as a bigger, darker and colder sound than its predecessor, praising Coldplay for showing a "new confidence" as well. This style was largely retained for their third album, *X&Y* (2005), albeit with the addition of electronic influences and extensive use of synthesizers, having a larger scale in terms of sound and existential themes.Craig McLean of *The Guardian* called it "the work of an increasingly motivated and forceful band," and described the tunes as "heartfelt material, with punchy guitar lines and emotive piano." The album's lyrics have been deemed to be "reflections on Martin's doubts, fears, hopes and loves," his words "earnest and vague, so listeners can identify with the underlying concepts in the songs."Kevin Devine of *Hybrid Magazine* wrote that Buckland's "shimmering guitar sound gives *X&Y* a euphonious glow," and thematically, the lyrics contain a "continuous thread of the importance of trying, as well as the need for basic communication amidst the cacophony of confusion in the world."

With *Viva la Vida or Death and All His Friends* and the subsequent *Prospekt's March - both* released in 2008 - Coldplay further diversified their style and explored new territories after completing what they saw as a trilogy of albums.The band experimented with many different instruments, including electric violins, tack pianos, *santoors* and orchestras, all while using more layered productions. They also tried different song structures and vocal identities at the suggestion of producer Brian Eno, taking influences from Eastern, Hispanic, African and Middle Eastern sounds.The title track, "Viva la Vida," is considered baroque pop and the fourth single "Strawberry Swing" was described as psychedelic-inspired. They also dabbled in *shoegaze on the* hidden track "Chinese Sleep Chant." The lyrics are more universal compared to previous material, and the subject matter is more collective as the band "delves into love, life, war and death." Martin commented that the motifs of the revolution were inspired by Victor Hugo's novel *Les Misérables* (1862).

Those themes, along with some of the Eastern influences, remained on 2011's *Mylo Xyloto*, a concept album that follows the story of two characters in the style of a *rock opera*. It broadened the spectrum of Coldplay's sound by including more electronic elements than before and featuring mostly upbeat tones for the first time, resulting in a pop *rock* style with "modern, urban, dance" tunes. According to Champion, the band originally wanted to make an acoustic album, so when "Paradise" began to take shape, they decided to start a separate electronic album. However, the two eventually became one body of work, with songs like "Charlie Brown" and "Us Against The World" reworked into their current versions. Berryman added that they approached the project with "a lot of confidence." As for the lyrics, Martin said he was inspired by old-school American graffiti, the White Rose movement and "being able to speak up or follow your passion, even if everyone seems to be against it." In 2013, a comic book based on the plot of the album was published in collaboration with Mark Osborne.

For *Ghost Stories* (2014), Coldplay adopted a brooding, melancholic style that is considered reminiscent of their debut, while incorporating electronic, R&B, *synth-pop* and *ambient* influences.Their melodies are also notably darker and more minimalist than *Mylo Xyloto*, with sparse arrangements that reflect their desire to "maintain a sense of space" without "being afraid of silence" or "layering too many sounds." The project is also considered a breakup album, lyrically exploring how past events in one's life-their ghosts-affect the present. Martin called it a "learning journey about unconditional love" after his divorce from Gwyneth Paltrow. A year later, *A Head Full of Dreams* was released in a similar style, but with bright, uplifting tones, contrasting with its predecessor and introducing elements of disco and *funk*, most notably on the single "Adventure of a Lifetime." In the lyrics they worked on themes of unity, dreaming, fatherhood, forgiveness, healing and gratitude.

In 2017, the band made *Kaleidoscope EP available* as a companion piece to the album. It included a live version of "Something Just Like This," their EDM collaboration with The Chainsmokers and Brian Eno's production on "Aliens."Meanwhile, tracks like "All I Can Think About Is You" and "Hypnotised" blended Coldplay's newfound pop style with their alternative *rock* roots, setting the template for *Everyday Life* (2019), which saw a return to the experimentation and organic sounds of *Viva la Vida or Death and All His Friends* while having new influences from gospel, *blues* and classical music.Released as the lead single along with "Orphans," the song "Arabesque" was inspired by *jazz* fusion and Afrobeat. The band continued their lyrical themes of positivity, equality, hope, legacy and humanity, but added loss, pain and commentary on political and social issues such as racism, police brutality, gun control and the refugee crisis, being their first album to feature profanity.

This multi-style approach was similarly present on 2021's *Music of the Spheres*, although it leaned toward pop sounds. According to Martin, the images of planets and space are a canvas for exploring the human experience: "It's really another record about living as a human person, but given this freedom that comes when you pretend it's about other creatures in other places." He was also inspired by the *Star Wars* film franchise, which made him wonder what other artists across the universe might be like after seeing the fictional Mos Eisley Cantina band perform. Champion further added that while *Everyday Life* was about "making the big questions personal," this album takes "the personal" and turns it "into big questions." New musical influences were noted on "Human Heart" and "Coloratura"; the former is an a cappella collaboration with R&B duo We Are King and Jacob Collier, while the latter is a progressive *rock* ballad that lasts 10 minutes and 18 seconds, making it the longest song the band has ever released.

Influences

Coldplay's music has been compared to A-ha, U2, Oasis, R.E.M. and Radiohead. They also acknowledge Scottish band Travis and American singer Jeff Buckley as major influences on their early material, which was primarily produced by Ken Nelson. Martin is known to be a fan of Bruce Springsteen, mentioned "spending three years trying to sound like Eddie Vedder" before Buckley, and commented that he listened to a lot of hymns when he was young due to his religious upbringing. During a 2021 interview, he cited Belgian singer-songwriter Stromae as another influence and noted that "he's one of our heroes, you know, he's one of those people that comes along and inspires you completely anew."

Buckland, on the other hand, claimed that The Stone Roses were one of the reasons he learned to play guitar. In 2020, he shared on social media playlists some of his favorite songs and artists from each decade, including The Velvet Underground, Carole King, Joy Division, Talking Heads, Kate Bush, Donna Summer, Björk, Beastie Boys and many others.He said during an interview the following year that his favorite song of all time is "Teardrop" by Massive Attack. Meanwhile, Berryman is known to draw inspiration from artists such as James Brown, Marvin Gaye, Kool & the Gang and The Funk

Brothers.He further added that his musical taste is "hard to sum up," but "I couldn't live without The Beatles or Motown." As for Champion, he commented that knowing how to play the violin and piano since he was eight years old gave him a different perspective on the drums, which he only learned to play after joining the band. During his youth, he listened to Bob Dylan, Tom Waits, Nick Cave and traditional Irish folk music. He has named Ginger Baker, Dave Grohl and John Bonham as some of his favorite drummers.

For *A Rush of Blood to the Head* (2002), they were inspired by Echo & the Bunnymen, George Harrison, and Muse. Their third studio album, *X&Y* (2005), was particularly influenced by Kraftwerk, Depeche Mode, and Johnny Cash. The song "'Til Kingdom Come" was originally written as a collaboration with the latter before he died. In addition to Nelson, the band also began working with Danton Supple for the album. On 2008's *Viva la Vida or Death and All His Friends*, Coldplay's style moved towards *art rock*, drawing inspiration from My Bloody Valentine, Blur, and Arcade Fire.After teaming up with Brian Eno and Jon Hopkins, they began to incorporate elements of *ambient* and electronic music into their compositions. The two producers returned on *Mylo Xyloto* (2011), although the former had a more direct role in helping to write the songs.

In 2014, *Ghost Stories* saw the group collaborate with Paul Epworth. Producers Tim Bergling and Madeon were also involved, resulting in some tracks having a "more danceable flavor," especially the single "A Sky Full of Stars." Released in 2015, *A Head Full of Dreams* featured producer/songwriting duo Stargate. Other longtime partners include Davide Rossi, Bill Rakho, Rik Simpson and Dan Green. The latter three are known as "The Dream Team" on *Everyday Life* (2019) and all four have been working with the band since *Viva la Vida or Death and All His Friends*. For their ninth album, *Music of the Spheres* (2021), Coldplay invited Max Martin. The song "People of the Pride" has an intro inspired by one of Beyoncé's performances at the Global Citizen Festival, while "Coloratura" generated comparisons to Pink Floyd.

Live presentations

Coldplay is known to "ensure that each tour is its own dazzling, illuminated spectacle," with their visual spectacles utilizing lasers, fireworks, confetti cannons and interactive LED wristbands, the latter of which is considered an iconic piece of their performances, as the band is credited with popularizing their use.Reviewing *Live in Buenos Aires* (2018), *Pitchfork*'s Sam Sodomsky stated that it "makes a strong case for the legacy of one of the 21st century's most enduring live acts," a perspective echoed by *The Guardian*'s Alexis Petridis after describing the band's setlists as "a bullish reminder of how [they] became, and then remained, huge." Both critics also commented on how Martin often interacts with the audience between each song's performance.

For Ghost Stories Tour, however, they performed intimate shows at venues such as the Royal Albert Hall and the Beacon Theatre. The concerts made use of new features including a laser harp and the reactable. A similar approach was taken for *Everyday Life* (2019) over their environmental concerns, with the band playing small shows for charity and a special live broadcast at the Amman Citadel in Jordan.Reviewing the latter, *NME*'s Dan Stubbs concluded that "on stage is where Coldplay come alive and where they make the most sense." In 2022, Champion said the Flaming Lips were instrumental in shaping his idea of how entertaining a concert can be, as the American band's tours have "a sense of wonder and fun that we really respond to."

Public image

Coldplay are considered polarizing pop *rock* icons, having received both praise and criticism from music critics and the public. They maintain a close relationship with fans through videos, letters and social media interactions, becoming the third and sixth most followed band in the world on Twitter and Instagram, respectively. They are also known to tease upcoming releases by spreading easter eggs and clues around the world.In a poll published by the *Daily Mirror* that listed the UK's most popular and unpopular artists, Coldplay were among the top 20 highest rated acts on both lists, the only other bands with the same distinction being ABBA and U2.In July 2000, Alan McGee described their songs as "bed-wetting music," a comment for which he later apologized in 2020, adding that "I don't like their music, but I don't think they're that bad." Buckland responded at the time by saying, "We're trying to be who we are, you know? To pretend to be 'a bit pissed off' would be sad."

Jon Pareles of *The New York Times* named Coldplay as "the most insufferable band of the decade," defining *X&Y* (2005) as "flawless to the extreme, with instrumental tracks purged of any hint of human frailty."In 2015, Carl Williott of Idolator compared it to the works of Phil Collins and noted that "such perfectionism was always considered cheesy in its day," but it had prestige in later eras "because the production values, songwriting and sheer talent stood the test of time."They were also accused of "sticking to a formula," to which some critics have argued that while Coldplay "never fully break with the conventions of a genre," they "travel" between them. Furthermore, while writing for *The Guardian*, Ben Beaumont-Thomas stated that "from genre-spanning albums to collaborating with Brian Eno and Beyoncé, they are far more radical than people realize," a sentiment echoed by *NME*'s Charlotte Krol while reviewing *Everyday Life* (2019).

Steven Hyden of Uproxx stated that Coldplay "will always be an irresistible target for a certain type of person" because they "represent mainstream pop *rock* more than any other act of the last twenty years," adding that "mainstream bands are the easiest musical entities to mock" and how "there is a presumption that there is nothing to 'get' with this band," but "if that were true, they wouldn't be so polarizing."Similarly, *The Independent* commented that they are "often positive, distinctly non-controversial and harmless," whereas "in the modern world - especially online - if you're not causing outrage, you might as well not exist."In a special editorial called "25 Songs That Tell Us Where Music Is Going," *The New York Times* selected "Hymn for the Weekend" and concluded that Coldplay's "widescreen pop brand attracts easy put-downs" like "edgeless" and "corny," but "like Phil Collins, Michael McDonald, ABBA or any number of hopelessly 'unfashionable' artists, their image will evaporate while their songs will stand the years," as the band "is built to endure."

Legacy

Recognitions and achievements

Coldplay is considered the most successful band of the 21st century. With over 100 million albums sold worldwide, they are one of the best-selling artists of all time. *Parachutes* (2000), *A Rush of Blood to the Head* (2002) and *X&Y* (2005) have all been included among the top 50 best-selling albums in UK history, marking the most appearances by a group in the ranking. The latter was the third fastest-selling album in the country since its release.In 2008, "Viva la Vida" became the first song by a British group to top the UK Singles Chart and *Billboard* Hot 100 since the Spice Girls' "Wannabe." Their lead album, *Viva la Vida or Death and All His Friends*, was the best-selling album of the decade in digital download formats. In 2013, *Forbes* named Coldplay as the most influential British celebrities in the world.The following year, they became the first band in history to surpass one billion plays on Spotify. Their performance at the 2016 Super Bowl 50 halftime show earned the largest audience for a band and a male act, and the impact of the event made them the most Googled band of the year. In November 2017, they wrapped up the A Head Full of Dreams Tour, currently the seventh highest grossing tour of all time.Coldplay then headlined Glastonbury Festival for a record-extending fifth time in 2021. During the same year, "My Universe" became the first song by a British band to debut at number one on *Billboard* Hot 100. In 2022, their tour gross surpassed US$1 billion from 12 million tickets sold at 456 reported shows, making them the fifth band in history to achieve the feat, after Bon Jovi, Eagles, The Rolling Stones and U2.

The band has also received numerous accolades throughout their career, becoming the most awarded and nominated group of all time at the Brit Awards - nine wins out of 30 nominations - and are the first act in history to win British Album of the Year three times and British Group four times, earning the most nominations for both categories.Coldplay also won seven Grammy Awards out of 39 nominations, receiving Song of the Year and Record of the Year once, while being nominated for Album of the Year three times. In January 2009, they received an NRJ Honor Award in recognition of their career achievements and impact. The band was then named Songwriters of the Year at the ASCAP London Music Awards the following year, having previously received the same honor from the Ivor Novello Awards in 2003.Their single "Atlas," which was released as part of the soundtrack to *The Hunger Games: Catching Fire* (2013), was nominated for the 19th Critics' Choice Awards and shortlisted for the 87th Academy Awards. In 2014, Coldplay was ranked as the sixth most awarded band of all time by *Fuse*.Two years later, the band was chosen for the NME Awards' Godlike Genius Award, which honors the "careers of music icons who have pioneered the industry." They have won two American Music Awards, seven *Billboard* Music Awards, seven MTV Video Music Awards, three Juno Awards, two silver awards at the Cannes Lions International Festival of Creativity and set 10 Guinness World Records, currently holding six of them. In May 2022, it was reported that the band's estimated combined wealth - without Harvey - exceeded £471 million.

Impact on music

According to Steve Baltin of *Forbes*, Coldplay has become the standard of today's alternative music scene and "through steady performance and adventurous work" continues to grow "into one of the best live bands in all of music." Writing for *Afisha*, Sergey Stepanov stated that they inherited U2's ability to "make alternative *rock* mainstream" and are "the Beatles of the 21st century" in terms of "hit-making skills and potential heft."In the Recording Academy's 20th anniversary review of *Parachutes* (2000), Jon O'Brien commented that the album "ushered in a new wave of mild-mannered guitar bands" and "helped open the floodgates for those who didn't subscribe to the *rock n' roll way* of thinking," impacting the work of groups like Fray, Snow Patrol and OneRepublic as well.Their hit single, "Yellow," is considered one of the best songs of the 2000s by *Pitchfork* and became part of the Rock and Roll Hall of Fame's "Songs That Shaped Rock and Roll" exhibit for being one of the most successful and important recordings in the music industry. Discussing key events in *rock* history, *The Guardian* commented that Coldplay set the direction of the genre for years to come with the song and brought a "fresh timbre of songwriting: wistful melancholy, buoyed by a sense of uplift."

Their second album, *A Rush of Blood to the Head* (2002), was chosen by Royal Mail for a series of labels celebrating classic British album covers of the last 40 years, also ranked as one of the best albums of all time by the Rock and Roll Hall of Fame, *NME*, and *Rolling Stone.*The latter magazine placed "Clocks" and "Fix You" at 490 and 392, respectively, on its list of "The 500 Greatest Songs of All Time." In 2010, Coldplay was included in VH1's "100 Greatest Artists of All Time" special, which recognized musical artists according to a survey of music industry experts.The following year, the band released *Mylo Xyloto*, which was added to *Q*'s editorial "The Best Albums of the Last 30 Years." Similarly, *Rolling Stone* ranked "Every Teardrop Is a Waterfall" among the best tracks of the 2010s, while "A Sky Full of Stars" was named one of the defining alternative *rock* songs of the period by iHeartRadio.The band is credited with boosting global exports of British music by the British Phonographic

Industry - BPI - along with Adele and Ed Sheeran, with 2016 and 2020 being the most notable years of contribution.

Meanwhile, Lakshmi Govindrajan Javeri of *Firstpost* stated that Coldplay has "mastered the art of reinvention" and consequently expanded "the list of artists inspired by them," resulting in the creation of "a rich multi-genre legacy."In addition, they are considered one of the most influential bands of the 21st century, impacting the work of artists such as Imagine Dragons, Halsey, The Killers, Avril Lavigne, Dua Lipa, Bruno Mars, Rammstein, Ed Sheeran, Harry Styles, Kanye West, and many others.In 2014, Bono commented that they were among the main influences for U2's thirteenth album, *Songs of Innocence*. Swedish producer and arranger Mattias Bylund explained that he made "Coldplay-like rhythmic chords" for Taylor Swift's "Wildest Dreams".American musician Finneas O'Connell cited the band as an inspiration for both his career and the production of Billie Eilish's debut album, *When We All Fall Asleep, Where Do We Go?* (2019). South Korean music director Lee Ji-soo said "Life in Technicolor II" was one of the songs that had an impact on the soundtrack for *In Our Prime* (2022).Writing for *G1*, Carol Prado mentioned that they helped reshape sertaneja music in Brazil, as several notable acts in the genre-including Luan Santana and Victor & Leo-were inspired by the band's use of "elongated syllables" and melodies that slowly "build up to strong choruses."Their music has been used on numerous occasions, including by Drake, Lizzo, Frank Ocean, and Chance the Rapper, while it has also been covered by singers such as Kelly Clarkson, Echosmith, Kacey Musgraves, Rosé, and Sam Smith.

Influence on live entertainment

Felipe Branco Cruz of *Veja* stated that Coldplay "reinvented the concept of *arena rock*," as their live performances turned fans into the protagonists of the show rather than mere spectators, continuing the legacy of shows "that transcend music" that was established by groups such as Pink Floyd, Queen, and U2. The band is also widely credited with popularizing the use of interactive LED wristbands at concerts.Acts that followed their trend include Lady Gaga, Taylor Swift, OneRepublic, The Weeknd, and Jay-Z. Jason Regler, the creator of the product, said his idea was conceived during a Coldplay performance. According to Didier Zacharie of *Le Soir*, the green plan proposed by the Music of the Spheres World Tour (2022-23) was "unprecedented" for a stadium tour, leading the band to be credited with "setting the blueprint" for environmentally friendly touring.In 2022, Live Nation's Lucy August-Perna commented that they helped further develop the framework the company had been developing over the previous five years and that their best practices and plans will be standardized to "provide sustainable touring options" for more artists. *Uproxx* and *Billboard* recognized Coldplay's impact on Happier Than Ever, Billie Eilish's The World Tour and Shawn Mendes' Wonder: The World Tour, respectively.Their work in partnership with John Wiseman - of Worldwide Sales - and Frederic Opsomer - of PRG Projects - for the LED stage elements resulted in the creation of products "that never existed before," such as inflatable three-dimensional orbs that "drastically" reduced the space needed to store and transport regular models. Opsomer also said the custom technology developed for the tour will become "commonplace in a few years" in the live entertainment industry, and thanked the band for "having the vision and backbone" of the effort.

Philanthropy

Coldplay donate 10 percent of all their profits to charities. The fund is held in a bank account that none of the members can access. The band currently supports over thirty organizations, including Amnesty International, Migrant Offshore Aid Station and Global Citizen Festival. They have spoken out about fair trade, supporting Oxfam's Make Trade Fair campaign by collecting over 70,000 signatures for their "Big Noise" petition on A Rush of Blood to the Head Tour and Twisted Logic Tour.In 2005, they partnered with the Make Poverty History movement and were featured in their campaigns. Coldplay also auctioned many significant memorabilia in 2009 for Kids Company, including Martin's first guitar, the globe from the *Parachutes* (2000) album cover and costumes worn during the Viva la Vida tour. The following year, they became sponsors of ClientEarth.

The band performed a slightly modified version of "A Message", titled "A Message 2010", on the television special Hope For Haiti Now, raising money for the victims of the 2010 Haiti earthquake. Berryman commented that "you can make people aware of the issues. It's not a lot of effort for us, if it can help people, then we want to do it." In 2012, Album Artists organized an exhibition composed of artwork from *Mylo Xyloto* (2011) in Camden, raised over £610,000 for Kids Company. Two years later, Martin joined the charity group Band Aid for a second time, performing alongside British and Irish acts in a new version of "Do They Know It's Christmas?" which raised money for the Ebola crisis in West Africa. In July 2017, the band made a donation of undisclosed value to the University of Southampton's Cancer Immunology Centre, which is the UK's first center dedicated to cancer immunology research.

Coldplay also contributed to Artists' Project Earth's *Plastic Oceans* album, the record was released on February 20, 2018 at the Ocean Plastics Crisis Summit in London, raising awareness and funds to counter plastic pollution.Under the pseudonym The Units, the band made *Global Citizen - EP 1 available* the same year, with royalties going towards the organization's education and advocacy efforts to end extreme poverty. In 2020, they released a music video for "Trouble In Town," inspired by George Orwell's *Animal Farm* (1944), and donated all proceeds from the broadcast and release to the Innocence Project and the African Children's Feeding Scheme.Coldplay also declared their support for The Ocean Cleanup project, sponsoring two boats that collect plastic from polluted rivers before it reaches the sea in Malaysia. As part of the band's efforts to make touring more sustainable, they announced a partnership with One Tree Planted, funding a tree for every ticket sold on Music of the Spheres World Tour through a global reforestation agreement. According to a report published by *The Times*, they donated more than £2.1 million to environmental causes through their J Van Mars Foundation during 2021.

Politics and activism

Martin, who lives in the United States, spoke out against the 2003 U.S.-led invasion of Iraq along with other military forces during a Teenage Cancer Trust concert at London's Royal Albert Hall, encouraging the crowd there to "sing against the war." He also showed his support for Democratic presidential candidates John Kerry in 2004 and Barack Obama in 2008.A year later, the band began participating in Meat Free Mondays, a food campaign started by Paul McCartney that seeks to help curb climate change by having at least one meat-free day a week. In 2011, Coldplay endorsed the song "Freedom for Palestine" by posting a link to the music video on their social media. They received more than 12,000 comments in less than a day, with fans agreeing or disagreeing with the message. Some threatened to boycott them and created a group demanding an apology from Israel. Eventually, the post was removed from their pages, however, OneWorld's Frank Barat stated that Facebook removed it after "thousands of people and computer-generated posts reported it as abusive," rather than the band's management.

Coldplay has also advocated for the LGBTQ community, which generated controversy with their performance at the Super Bowl 50 halftime show. Conservatives accused the band of promoting the "gay agenda" late in the show, where the audience flipped rainbow-colored banners reading "Believe in Love."They were also among the artists who signed a public letter of support for the Equality Act in the U.S. In June 2016, Coldplay was in favor of "Vote Remain" in the U.K.'s European Union membership referendum. Following the Brexit result, in which 52% of the country voted to leave the European Union despite the majority of young people voting to remain, Martin commented that "this decision does not represent us or the majority of our generation or the generation that follows us." A year later, they performed at Ariana Grande's One Love Manchester benefit concert, which was organized in response to the Manchester Arena bombing and raised funds to help the victims of the attack, as well as their families.Months later, they performed as special guests at the Concert for Charlottesville following the events of the Unite the Right rally. In November 2019, the band released *Everyday Life*, in which they more prominently expressed their stance against racism, police brutality and gun violence.Two years later, they were among the artists who signed a public letter endorsing the Equality Act. In 2023, the Malaysian Islamic Party attempted to cancel the band's concert at the Bukit Jalil National Stadium, as Martin often waves the rainbow flag while performing.

Promotions

Despite their worldwide popularity, Coldplay has remained notoriously protective of how their material appears in the media. The band regularly allows songs to be used in movies and television shows, but commercials are limited to very rare occasions. In 2002, it was reported that they turned down more than $85 million in contracts from companies such as Gatorade, Diet Coke and Gap. Martin said, "We couldn't live with ourselves if we sold the meanings of the songs that way."The first time one of their songs was used for advertisements was with "Viva la Vida" in 2008, the band signed a contract with Apple and promoted the exclusive availability of the single on iTunes. In 2010, Martin appeared at the company's September event. After Steve Jobs' death, Coldplay performed four tracks at the Apple Campus, posthumously thanking him for his support.

Six years later, they participated in a Target commercial promoting the exclusive deluxe edition of *Ghost Stories* (2014). Meanwhile, the music video for "Adventure of a Lifetime," which was directed by Mat Whitecross and shot at The Imaginarium, had a product placement from Beats. The company was allowed to use some parts of the video in their commercials as a reward for covering the budget. In 2018, director Jon M. Chu revealed that he sent a letter directly to the band outlining all of his reasons for getting permission to use "Yellow" in *Crazy Rich Asians*.

In 2021, Coldplay announced a major partnership with German multinational BMW as part of its efforts to make touring as sustainable as possible. They said the company's technology, which includes the world's first recyclable automotive batteries, can power live performances almost entirely with renewable energy.As part of the deal, the band contributed to the marketing of two of the company's electric cars and allowed "Higher Power" to be used in commercials. In 2022, DHL became Coldplay's transportation partner for the Music of the Spheres world tour (2022-23) due to the company's "expertise and investment in sustainable logistics" and transportation solutions.

Members

- Chris Martin - lead vocals, keyboards, piano, rhythm guitar, harmonica (1996-present)
- Jonny Buckland - lead guitar, backing vocals, keyboards (1996-present)
- Will Champion - drums, backing vocals, keyboards, piano, percussion (1996-present)
- Guy Berryman - bass, backing vocals, keyboards, synthesizers, percussion (1996-present)

- Phil Harvey - manager (1998-2002), creative director (2006-present)

Discography

- 2000: *Parachutes*
- 2002: *A Rush of Blood to the Head*
- 2005: *X&Y*
- 2008: *Viva la Vida or Death and All His Friends*
- 2011: *Mylo Xyloto*
- 2014: *Ghost Stories*
- 2015: *A Head Full of Dreams*
- 2019: *Everyday Life*
- 2021: *Music of the Spheres*

Filmography

- 2006: *How We Saw the World*
- 2011: *American Express Unstaged*
- 2018: *Coldplay: A Head Full of Dreams*
- 2019: *Everyday Life - Live in Jordan*
- 2020: *Coldplay: Reimagined*

- 2021: *Live from Climate Pledge Arena*
- 2022: *Live Broadcast from Buenos Aires*
- 2023: *Live at River Plate*

Music tours

- Parachutes Tour (2000-2001)
- A Rush of Blood to the Head Tour (2002-2003)
- Twisted Logic Tour (2005-2007)
- Viva la Vida Tour (2008-2010)
- Mylo Xyloto Tour (2011-2012)
- A Head Full of Dreams Tour (2016-2018)
- Music of the Spheres World Tour (2021-2023)

Other books by United Library

https://campsite.bio/unitedlibrary

Milton Keynes UK
Ingram Content Group UK Ltd.
UKHW020853131123
432470UK00021B/1120